Wings

Poems

Shirin Ramzanali Fazel

Copyright © 2017 by Shirin Ramzanali Fazel

Wings - Poems

All rights reserved. No part of this publication may be reproduced or transmitted in any form by any means, electronic or mechanical, including photocopying, recording or any information storage or retrieval system, without the prior permission in writing from the Author.

ISBN-13: 978-1544811963
ISBN-10: 1544811969

Published in the UK

Cover Photograph mariobadagliacca2013 - Lampedusa
Cover Design Gianmarco Mancosu

*To all the Birds with
broken Wings*

Contents

Diaspora
    Love Letter to My Hometown 3
    Women on a Cat Walk 5
    Heritage 8
    Friends 10
    Neighbourhood 12
    Afka Hooyo - Mother Tongue 16

Caught in the Middle
    Alien 21
    Blue Gazebo 23
    Father 26
    Ghost City 28
    Hero 30
    Postcard 33
    Stubbornness 34
    Twiga - Giraffe 36
    Underground 38
    Walls 40
    Wings 42

Migrants
    Borders 45
    Children of the World 47
    Clessidra 48
    If We Knew ... But We Know! 50
    Insane? 52
    Mare Nostrum 53
    Mother 57
    Pick and Choose 58
    Shambles 59

    About the Author 61

Diaspora

LOVE LETTER TO MY HOMETOWN

Kuala Lumpur: January 20, 2017

Assalamu' Alaikum Wa Rahmatuullahi Wa Barakatuh
May Peace and Mercy and the Blessings of Allah be upon you

My beloved Xamar,

> Yours was the first air I breathed
> The first blue sky my eyes gazed on
> I daydreamed watching your white and pink clouds
>
> Like *hooyo* - mother you nourished me
> Our lively ancient neighbourhood protected me
> *Abti* - Uncle, *habaryar* - auntie and *ayeeyo* - grandmother
> None of them tied to me by blood
> Made me feel I belonged to a large noisy *reer* - family

I treasure
The voices, the scent and the taste of Boondheere,
Via Roma, Shingaani, Xamar Weyne and the Tamarind market

In exile on lonely nights
I have longed for
Your warm salty ocean waves
And the slightly fermented taste of *caano geel* - camel milk

> I wept bitter tears
> When I saw you bleeding
> And my large noisy family
> Wounded, maimed, killed

Shirin Ramzanali Fazel

Mogadishu
Like a lost child I dream of you
My heart will never fall in love again

You only you
Can make me cry, laugh,
Bring back memories of my childhood
The pain of the present
And hope for a better future

>   We belong to each other,
>   My beloved Xamar

Shirin Ramzanali Fazel

WOMEN ON A CATWALK

Faded pictures hidden in my memories
Like black and white photos
Hooyo wearing an off the shoulder *guntiino*
Hand made cotton *alindi*
Wrapped around her waist
Her slim bare arms holding me
Her hair bundled in a bright red *shaash*
Her familiar smell of aromatic *cuunsi* and sweat
Soothing my whims

She tells me
This *guntiino* carries a long history
When a woman was free and protected
A nomad woman nourishing her children
Looking after her goats and sheep
Building her own *aqal* shelter
A strong hard-working woman
Carrying water harvesting crops
Pounding maize for preparing *soor* cornmeal
Simple fulfilling comfort food
Soo mal camel milk
Known for centuries
Rich in vitamins protein and healing properties

I treasure my trunk filled with memorabilia
Old picture postcards of *bellissime* brown girls
Wearing *guntiino* and amber necklaces
Advertising sweet bunches of bananas from Somalia
For the Italian market

When I was a child women wore *guntiino*
Walking on busy streets
Draped in light rainbow cotton
They stroll on Lido Beach
Gentle ocean waves slapping their feet

In my teenage years a western wind blows
I see sleeveless frocks and bell bottom jeans
Soon forgotten
There is no beauty and national pride

Diaphanous *dirac* became the popular one
One size fits all
Loose and transparent enhances femininity
Mix and match with *gorgorad* underskirt
Made of silk embroidered in gold
Mix and match with pink and orange *garbasaar* shawls
That veil bosom and the coolest hair trends

I walk the streets of London and Cape Town
Cities oppressed by fashion billboards
I meet women wearing black and brown *jalabeeb*
They are covered from head to toe
Not tempted by designer clothes
Except for their Clarks and Nike trainers

I can spot them from afar
They are not invisible
Their presence is real
They mingle they shop they walk the streets
They travel they vote they trade
They integrate
They do not assimilate

They want to make a statement
They do not want to fade away
To blend to compromise
They want to protect
Scattered families
Culture tradition language
Faith
Identity

Under the *jalabeeb*
They conceal their beauty
Smooth skin perfumed with
Jasmine and red rose
Fragrant *bhakhour* and musk
They wear *guntiino* and *dirac*
They play with colours
Pink orange red turquoise
Huruud turmeric yellow
and *buluug* blue
Bright jewellery and bold hairstyles

HERITAGE

    People lost the memory of how it all began
    They just kept passing it on for generations.

    Others say it all began at the time
    When Pharaoh ruled the land of Thebes
    Tradition travelled on the shoulders of the river Nile

    It slithers silent, calm, sometimes angry
    Coursing through different lands
    Whispering to peasants and nobles.

        Darkness sneaks into the hearts of men.

    The screams, the pain, the sadness never spared
    Your loving grandmother, your mother
    Your sister, your aunt.

        My body aches at the sight of the sharp knife
    Knowing no mother would stay still
    And swallow bitter tears
    If only she could choose -
    She is crushed under
    Layers and layers of blindness

        While her little girl,
    Knees apart, is CUT, CUT, CUT.

Now you know
It does not have to do with Islam
It is when people get confused, mixed up.

Thank you, mother,
For breaking the silence:
Now I can dance with the wind
Like papyrus on the banks
Of the river Nile

FRIENDS

Little girls playing with an old plastic doll
Pretending to be mothers -
Cuddling and feeding is their favourite game...
They giggle, they comb each other's hair.
Soft feet stamp in dusty alleys
Where cats sleep and play hide and seek.

School days are fun
Then comes the time for exams:
They are a team, they struggle and they succeed.
Seasons pass, they share *cuuns* - incense and *cillaan* - henna
Comes the time to have a family,
Looking after babies is not just fun:
Sleepless nights, a new tooth and tummy ache -
They can count on each other,
They share secrets, recipes and fairy tales.

The city is swallowed in chaos:
People are fleeing, people are looting.
No more *nabad* - peace -
And no more chit chat - *sheeko sheko* -
Everything is lost!

Like beggars in a new city -
Hearts bursting with sorrow,
Eyes full of tears from the bitter cold,
Dragging a bunch of children to school
Preparing them for a new life,
A different culture, a different language -
Soor, ambulo, anjero, bariis iskukaris iyo moos

Are exotic Somali food...
MacDonald's is now their favourite place:
Chicken and chips,
Fish and chips...
Play stations and video games
Become real friends.

Cooking, cleaning,
Pulling shopping trolleys -
It's a full time job,
No neighbour to share a pot of shah with...

Double-decker buses
Jammed with people,
Tight jeans, leggings and black *abayas*...
Mobile phones ring,
Dialects travelling from far lands
Mix and dance in the air...

Her Samsung rings -
It's her umbilical cord -
A familiar voice showers her with joy:
'Abaayo, arurta goorme fasax so qaadaneysa?' -
'Sister when are the children coming for their holiday?'
These words, full of sunshine, bring to life
The little girls playing with the old plastic doll.

NEIGHBOURHOOD

I grew up in a neighbourhood
With people I knew
Uncles and aunties
With no blood ties

Sharing biscuits and *chai*
Laughter and
Sheko-sheko chit-chat

Funerals, and marriages
Exchanging gifts
Sharing sweets: *Xalwo, Shuushuumow, Gashaato* coconut cake

The beggars I knew
The milk woman
The vegetable man
The street cats

Today I live in a neighbourhood where everything is vague
From my kitchen window
Washing dishes
I watch my neighbours passing by

The grandmother in a tracksuit
With her thick grey bun
Cuddling her granddaughter
The little girl I see
Growing day by day
But I don't know
When her birthday is

The bachelor who got married
The house lit in orange red and green
Loud music and fancy cars
Ladies in shining silk frocks
Men wearing crowns

I watch the Afghan mother
Scuttling along
With her three little ones
She is rushing,
Hurrying them to school

The tall lonely lad with his big Afro
The blonde Bulgarian girl in stilettos walking proudly
The three Middle-Eastern ladies chatting through the *nikab*
The wonky legged man carrying his heavy shopping bag
The cheeky chubby girl with her dangling pony tail

Every day the same people
Walk, stroll stride past

They are familiar faces
I wish I knew them well
I give them names and imagine their … stories

Grandma Anita is carrying her grandchild Anju
Who is two years old
'They grow up so fast' she whispers in her heart

On Sundays Sunil wearing his trendy track suit
Drives his bride in his red Fiesta
To feast on *paratha* and *daal*
Comfort food that only taste so good
when it is home cooked
By his mother

Leila her lips sucked in is scuttling down Cape Hill
But her heart is in Kabul
Her three pretty daughters
Bilqis, Bibi and Beena
Have never flown a kite
Standing on the roof of the house
Where she was born

The handsome young lad
Reminds me of Malcolm X
With a meaningful expression
Stamped on his face
I call him Malcolm

Nikol has chosen her romantic look
Her high heels click clack as she walks down the street
Her head up in the sky absorbed in her dreams
She is asking the clouds 'Where is my Nikolai
My high school sweetheart?'

Marwa, Jamila and Huda exchange the latest news
From their families in Yemen
Blinking their eyes
Red rimmed from their sleepless nights
'They have no water supply'
'When will these atrocities end?'
'My uncle was killed'

Winston is wearing his oversize grey coat
He is dragging his shopping bag
He is heading for his empty house

Kate capering on her chubby young legs
With her dangling pony tail is
Sharing her big smile with us
She brings sunshine to our neighbourhood

Every day the same people
Walk stroll stride past

Shirin Ramzanali Fazel

AFKA HOOYO - *Mother Tongue*

The sounds I carry in my memories:
I live in this bubble of voices -
The sweet warm milk suckled from *hooyo's* generous breast,
My falling into sleep covered in a blanket of words...

My first steps: I wobble, I fall, salty tears ploughing down my face...
I look at the blue sky,
I stutter, struggle - a funny sound ...
Hooyo laughs - she giggles ...
She makes me repeat the same word again and again.
Her eyes flicker like the first stars that peep in the inky night.

The sound of this language has memories
Built brick by brick,
It can move my deepest emotions -
The hidden ones
Like pearls buried at the bottom of the sea.
This language is not always
Mellow, pure, soft, musical, kind -
This same language
Can hurt, curse, wound my heart and leave invisible scars:
These guttural harsh sounds can heal my soul.

I carry these notes like a timeless instrument:
I am the howling sound of the arid desert wind,
The pungent scent of the bush,
The early raindrops of *Gu* and *Dayr* - spring and autumn,
I am the music of camel bells marching towards abundance,

I am the cracking sound of charcoal burning *lubaan* -
frankincense,
I am the frail sobbing of a moaning tribe,
Of a child crying for help...
I am the ruthless echo of uninvited bullets,
Of hatred and destruction,
I am the bitter soul whispering prayers...

I struggle when I have to read this language I love most,
Written in an alphabet adopted from a foreign land,
Signs not strong enough to lift my heavy tongue -
I feel like a ballerina dancing on a broken toe.
I abandon this newspaper,
I refuse to read these words:
Burcad badeed, burbur, baahi, argagixiso, cadow -
Pirates, destruction, poverty, terrorism, enemy...
Dagaal, dhimasho, dhiig -
War, death, blood...

I treasure the language of poets:
Hooyo's lullabies,
Jokes and proverbs...
Blessings and goodness -
Barako iyo wanaag

Caught in the Middle

ALIEN

    Where is home?
    The land I left behind?
    The tears that flooded my chest
    And tore at my mother's guts?

    It's the shadows I left behind
    Shrouded in a smoke of guilt
    Scorching my limbs

    It's the faceless child
    Haunting my nights

        Where is home now?
        It's the blistering desert wind enraging my thirst

        Was it the biting numbing sea
        That butchered my thoughts?

Where is home?
My thoughts hang on a string
Blown by a howling storm

Where is home?
An unfamiliar country
Covered in hail

        I grieve like
        A defeated boxer
        Alien words punch
        My ugly face

Silently I bleed
I weep
I wail

Like a rhino -
Trapped

BLUE GAZEBO

A blue gazebo stands on the beach
Three boys wearing red white and blue flowered Bermuda
  shorts
Are sleeping after a long night
Of hustling and music

The early morning sun
Squeezes its rays through the sky
The sea is calm
Blue smooth as velvet
Gentle waves playing music

A family with a toddler
Splash in the water
Three old men
With flabby muscles
Walk slowly along in the sea
All of them wearing white hats
They chat
Like sitting in a café

Few people on the beach
At this early hour
Time passes slowly
People come
Eyes searching for a place
Like birds nesting
They sit and create boundaries
And declare their territory

It is August high season
They want to choose the best spot
A man with a thick white beard
Is carrying a long branch from a palm tree
He digs a hole in the sand and sticks the branch in

A noisy family arrives
The man is carrying two heavy cool bags
The woman is holding a green plastic alligator
For her youngest child
The others are carrying beach umbrellas
A chubby puppy trotting behind them

Two teenagers are playing table tennis
They hit the ball frantically
Only the harsh sound of the ball on the wooden bats

A lonely boy with brown skin is kicking a white ball
A woman is dipping her crying daughter in the sea

There is laziness in the air
The sun warms every pore
A couple wearing matching hats stroll by
She is covered with a black and green burkini

The sound of the waves
And footsteps of children running on the shore
Mix like a natural orchestra

A group of cheerful women
Wearing colourful burkini
Walk out of the water
Their voices rise from the sea
French and Arabic mingle in the air

The sun's rays play golden and silver
The soft white sand mapped with footsteps
The blue sky touches the blue sea
The three boys are still sleeping under the gazebo
Only the hot sun is a reminder that the day is lengthening

At the end of the bay
Tall white buildings
Mark the new development for tourist
Empty rooms
Filled with ghosts
After the attack on the Mediterranean beach

FATHER

Father you have always been there for me
Working night shifts
Always present
Proud of my school grades

Hiding your foreign accent
You pushed me so hard
To learn to be better than the others

We are in England now
We must speak English
You are British
Is your motto

Libraries become my playground
Books my favourite friends
You changed my name
'It is for your own good'
'What is the use of having a long name
Difficult to pronounce?'

I cried in smelly school loos
Beaten and bullied
Because I was not one of them

'Dad teach me your language'
I begged you
'This language is no good to you
It belongs to forgotten villages
This is your home now'

Home?
Even now I don't know where home is
Graffiti on the walls
Suspicious looks from my colleagues
When terror hits the news

GHOST CITY

Roaming like a tabby cat in an unfamiliar neighbourhood
I grasp my red leather bag
Cold air plays through my red hair
No sunshine for days
Only rain dripping onto my red umbrella

At the bus stop
A woman is wrapped from head to toe
In a black cloak
Her bare hands tattooed in dark henna
She is talking on the phone
A grating guttural sound
Gushing from her throat

I shiver at the penetrating sound
Like scratches on my scalp
I bleed for my mother tongue

Is this the country
I was dreaming of?
Is this really England?

The bus driver is wearing a red turban
A thick grey moustache entangles his bushy beard
Sad dark circles under his eyes glued to the road
Punjab smouldering on his face

On the bus
I am immersed in a cacophony of voices
Overlapping words
Terrified like a lost inky crow
I fly on barren lands
Dried-up rivers empty villages

I sit with my stomach tight
Next to me a man folding his body in despair
He smells of urine and alcohol
Fragile bony hands holding a brown bag

Rain drops slide on the window
I remember my Greek island buried in sunshine
I swathe my woollen scarf around my neck
I get off in a stream of people

HERO

He wears a military uniform
Sitting legs stretched
In a protected bunker

His sharp eyes spy
Glued to the screen
Only the flickering green light
Lights the room

His hand
Does not shake
Does not sweat
He is trained
He is skilled at video games
He has won many competitions

He knows when to shoot the target
He gets points
He is a hero

His gaze falls on
Moving shadows
These silhouettes walk
But he can't hear their footsteps

>They breathe
>But he can't hear their breath
>They talk
>But there are no voices

He can't see
The white bearded grandfather
Carrying his thousand wishes
And sweetest joys
Folded in the geography
Of his expression

He can't see
The young farmer's
Silky hair covering his upper lips
And the glint of spring dreams
Moulding his smile

He can't see
Lively cheerful children kicking the ball in the yard
He can't see
The woman's hands frying onions

> His thumb is impatient
> He presses the button on the joystick
> A violent blast
> Scatters roofs, tiny arms
> Turbans beds goats
> To bury them under rubble

No sound in the room
His shift is over

He drives home in a black GMC pick up
The local radio station babbles
The weather forecast
The latest sport
And the top Oscar nominee

POSTCARDS

    Tourist travel and see places
    Take selfies and send photos
    Buckingham Palace is where the tour starts
    Piccadilly Circus Tower of London
    They browse at stalls in Portobello Market
    They shop at Harrods
    Even if they only buy a small bag with the name on
    To show off 'I have been to London.'

    Postcards you don't see
    Creepy neighbourhoods
    Dirty alleys
    Mothers struggling to feed babies
    Drug addicts selling their soul

    Tourist travel and see places
    Take selfies and photos
    Piazza San Pietro, Fontana di Trevi
    Il Colosseo, Porta Portese
    Young lovers rest on Piazza di Spagna's steps
    For a romantic kiss and a cuddle

    Postcards you don't see
    Hidden behind the kitchen of expensive restaurants
    Exploited migrant workers
    With swollen feet and numb fingers
    Picking tomatoes and watermelons
    In slavery

Shirin Ramzanali Fazel

STUBBORNNESS

I got into trouble in school
My small arms knotted around my waist
I sweat trying to translate
The teacher's words

Mother you are not familiar
With this foreign language

Mother your round dark face
Watching me
Your piercing pitch-dark eyes
Reading my thoughts
Like a simple book

    I lower my gaze
    I am too proud to lie

Your guttural voice
Gets muffled
Your inquisitive eyes become slits
You clench your fits
Bite your upper lip

    My tongue is like a contortionist
    Twisting rolling pulling
    That magic muscle

I look at the teacher
Her mouth like a whistling kettle
Words flow

    I try to translate
    But the words are too long
    I waver can't find a good match
    My mind is wandering

    I swallow the words
    Stuck in my throat
    My tummy groans
    I hold my bladder

Sunshine is knocking boldly on the window
I hear the chirping voices of children playing
I imagine white-grey feathered seagulls
Sleeping on the slippery roof

Shirin Ramzanali Fazel

TWIGA - *Giraffe*

At Dudley Zoo I ran into
Your begging wailing eyes
Under a mocking steel sky

You camouflage your melancholy
Behind stunning strong legs and
Thick long black lashes

We speak the same tongue
The language of the land
We left behind

I can stroke your pain
I know how shattered you are
You walk toward me
You crane
Your slim triangle head
Brush against the wired fence

Your smoky breath
Whispers and sighs

> Where are my sisters?
> Are they mating and munching
> Under our blue sky?

With a pain inside me
I glide to the time
When eight of us
Had fun chasing pink clouds

    We were all young and alive
    Dressed for a party
    Laughing at funny creatures

    Who obsessively snap
    Stealing the moment
    To store in a box

While the wild wind whistles
Over acacia trees and
Bushy Wonderland.

UNDERGROUND

People like giant ants buried in the ground
Rush around anxiously following signs
Brown red green pink lines
Metallic crackling voices announce arrivals
No blinding sunshine filters from these man-made tunnels

People lost in their hangover dreams
Grasp for a fake Paradise
Pushing their lives to the limit
Swathed in winter clothes
Isolated and deaf to humanity
Earphones plugged to secure their world

People packed in disorderly claustrophobic spaces
Eyes dart deliberately avoiding contact
Hands grip swinging handles
Legs tight to the swaying ground
Hearts locked in an inescapable darkness

People stealthily checking
A suspect face
Fear plays nasty games

Young male
Thick black beard
Brown skin tone
Carrying a rucksack
The enemy is among us

Squeezed into this hostile atmosphere
A young woman prays in silence
For her safe return home
Her headscarf is a heavy flag to carry

WALLS

Walls
Invisible walls
Resistant like bulletproof glass
Cage us everyday

Walls
Created by tragic events
Suspicious looks
Blasphemous words
Hysterical reaction

Walls
The result of howled orders
Given by greedy ships' captains
Who abruptly change course
 Just to satisfy their own needs

Walls
Built on the lies of jokes
Eager to perform on a worldwide stage

Walls
Piled up by words that brand the flesh
Persistent slogans endlessly repeated
Newspaper headlines relentlessly sowing
Phrases borrowed from talk shows
Words bouncing and spurting
Like molten metal

Walls
Barricades of barbed wire
Strangling our emotions
Hearts bleeding in silence

'Us and them'

WINGS

I lost the memory of my birthplace
Irreplaceable taste of honey
From her loving hand
Whispers of tales and lullabies

I watch an old flag hanging on the wall
Faded photos in cheap wooden frames

I carry my rainbow feathers
Like an exotic bird
I fly over monotonous cities
Polluted lakes
Melting icebergs
Burning forest

I hear loud voices
Of hatred and violence
And racist remarks

I pray for love
Justice
And peace for
All the other
Birds with broken wings

Migrants

BORDERS

From the Alps
To Copenhagen
Chocolates travel - lavishly
Designer bags travel - extravagantly
Cheese and wine travel - abundantly
Across borders

Across borders
From shelled homes
Scattered limbs
And burnt fields

Young men escape with broken spirits
Women choke clutching their children
Shuffling bleeding feet in the wilderness

The haggard old man
Bites his lips
Wrapped in a rough blanket
Hiding his despair

Bellies rumbling
Hungry for soup
Children shiver and sob
For a snug bed

Lifeless eyes sunken in their sockets
Howls of horror
And the ugly bitter taste of defeat
Whirl in their skulls

    They march
    They walk
    They trudge

To reach barbed-wire fences
Where soldiers hold guns
To defend the border

CHILDREN OF THE WORLD

"Migrant" "*extracomunitario*"
Words echo across the media
Words not like the sound
Of birds' wings
But like a bitter brand burnt into people's skin

The infinite blue sky
No borders no guns no documents
Birds are free to fly

"Migrant" "*extracomunitario*"
A heavy necklace to carry when you enter
The European Union
A stamp that sticks
To your children and their children to come

My childhood was safe
Never met a "migrant" "*extracomunitario*"
Only people
Who spoke different languages
A festival of colours
A festival of food
A festival of music
Ring a Ring-o' Rosie *Giro-Giro-Tondo*
Holding hands and singing all together

Shirin Ramzanali Fazel

CLESSIDRA

We flee from icy weather
Traffic jams and boring jobs
Long queues at supermarkets and cinemas

We flee from congested malls
Christmas trees with empty souls
And crammed underground trains

Jambo - welcome!
Golden beaches where the sun turns our pale skin lobster-colour
Warm sea waves invigorate our stiff muscles

Vivid yellow and green wristbands
Promote us to a high caste
A sign of privilege 'All inclusive'
Free lager at the pool bar
Lavish lunch-buffet
And 'yummy' barbecues at sunset!

-

They flee from hungry growling dogs
From piles of rotting garbage
From man hunting man
And stark winds whistling through empty swings
In abandoned parks

They flee from empty shops
Endless lines of cars at petrol stations
Shelled buildings
And mass graves

Welcome to a frowning police border control
Long hours squatting on interview chairs
Registration humiliation classification
Dehumanisation

Shivering bones ache for sunshine
Light bulbs hang from the ceiling
Healthy skin decays into lizard scales

Bright red wristbands
Degrade them to a lower caste
'Asylum seekers'

IF WE KNEW ... BUT WE KNOW !

We are bombarded by images
We are buried in newspapers
We are stretched like an elastic band
In talk shows
To decide
Who are the good guys
And who are the bad guys

Our safety comes first
How to defend our borders
To protect our culture
To preserve our religion
Our heritage
Our freedom

At Summits
Politicians
Spend time talking
Showing their muscles
At tables garnished
With fresh cut flowers
Drinking clean Evian water

They shake hands
Sign agreements
Fly back home safely
In private jets

Every decision is about us
We are narrow minded
Egocentric

Fortress Europe
History never forgets
The shadows of the past

INSANE ?

Insane?
Who is insane
To leave behind
Home
Family
Neighborhood
And friends?

Who wants
To be beaten
To be raped
In the desert
Or die in the sea?

When our sea feeds
The rich
When our oil
Generates wealth

When our land
Is being polluted
When our
Children starve
To death

MARE NOSTRUM

Mare Nostrum
Sunshine and Riviera
Restaurants sun beds and *gelato*
Women topless and in bikinis
Sunscreen and waterproof mascara

Mare Nostrum
Boats small boats big boats
Packed with people with brown skin
Who are they?
'Immigrati' is their label
Greedy creatures who are after our way of life

Mare Nostrum
The Mediterranean diet to live longer
Olive oil pasta and fresh salad
A glass of vintage red wine to keep the heart pumping

Mare Nostrum
Giant hungry beast
Which feeds on human flesh
What's on the menu makes no difference
Young men children pregnant women
The required ingredients:
They must be desperate fleeing from chemical weapons
Political oppression civil war and starvation

Shirin Ramzanali Fazel

Mare Nostrum
Romans ancient monuments
Testimony of great civilizations
Great history great architecture
Every century is dated preserved in museums
Expert archaeologists dig dust catalogue
Search for the glorious past

Mare Nostrum
News what's on the news?
No news it's everyday news
Today a boat sank seven hundred migrants drowned
Last week a boat sank four hundred migrants drowned
On New Year's Eve a boat sank five hundred migrants drowned
We do not have the exact figure
Last year approximately three thousand migrants drowned

Mare Nostrum
Resorts cosy guest houses and hotels
Bookings are required
Name address and credit card number
Lavender - scented bed linen is tucked into King-sized beds
Dining rooms set with silver polished cutlery and champagne glasses
On coffee tables fresh cut flowers
Smile as guests to arrive.

Mare Nostrum
Quiet hush keep quiet
People are dying
No names no faces no numbers no graves
No trace
They vanish they disappear

Mare Nostrum
Talk politicians talk
Debate debate debate
Help! European Union help
Elections
Vote for me
I will keep you safe from barbaric invasion

Mare Nostrum
Blame unscrupulous traffickers
Let's go after them

The human traffickers are responsible
Let's have a naval blockade
Point our missiles toward them

Mare Nostrum
We have got amnesia no memory of yesterday
Fascist propaganda says that we export civilization
The reality is that we conquer massacre divide grab resources
Today we export "democracy"
The reality we use dictators
When we do not need them
We bomb them and their whole country
We make money selling obsolete weaponry
We have drones we experiment on the ground
We create death agony displacement
Justified as collateral damage

Mare Nostrum
Silence only a vast blue sea
Silence broken by the noise of crushing waves
Silence people keep silent
No words
To honour the dead

MOTHER

Mother
I look at you
You are shaped
Like a womb

You are warm
Loving
Generous

You have been chained
Raped
Exploited

You did not cry
You gave
And gave more

You are the endless pot
Where greedy fingers
Dig for more

Shirin Ramzanali Fazel

PICK AND CHOOSE

Pick and choose
Like cattle
Fit for the market

Endless documents
Forms
Questionnaires
To be filled

It is your colour
That says it all

You are not good enough
You are young strong
You have brains
To become someone
If only you had the chance

You are not good enough
You want to live
You want to work
You want to have a family

You are not good enough
You are 'black'!
Go back!

SHAMBLES

    Endings
    Come by surprise
    And they can be
    The worst nightmare

    Your home pounded to the ground
    By an enemy you have never met
    The lush pomegranate tree
    You planted for your son Sami
    Burnt out
    Its branches spread
    Lifeless
    Its red flowers
    Scattered like blood

        Your loving wife Wafaa
        Your devoted mother
        Your sleek dark haired child Hannah
        Buried under rubble

    When your fingers bleed
    And your heart pleads
    When your tears flow dry
    And your tongue is thirsty

        When pigeons don't coo
        When all the air stinks
        When kites don't fly
        And church bells don't chime

    How do you begin?

Shirin Ramzanali Fazel

ABOUT THE AUTHOR

Shirin Ramzanali Fazel is an Italian writer of Somali and Pakistani origins. Shirin was born in Mogadishu, Somalia, where she attended Italian schools. In 1971, she left her country and she arrived in Novara, Italy. Shirin has lived in several countries including Zambia, the United States, Kenya, Saudi Arabia, and Tunisia. She currently lives in Birmingham, United Kingdom. Her first novel *Lontano da Mogadiscio* (Rome: Datanews 1994) is considered a milestone of Italian postcolonial literature and it describes her experience of migration to Italy and the effects of Italian colonialism in her native country. Shirin's second novel, *Nuvole sull'Equatore* (Cuneo: Nerosubianco, 2010) deals with the issue of *meticciato* and race discrimination, a crude legacy of the Italian colonial government. *Lontano da Mogadiscio/ Far from Mogadishu*, an extended and bilingual version of the 1994 edition was published in 2013 by Laurana as an e-book. In 2016, Shirin published the English translation of *Far from Mogadishu* in a printed form.

Shirin Ramzanali Fazel has as well published several short stories and poems in various anthologies and magazines. She is part of the advisory board of the Arts and Humanities Research Council funded project 'Transnationalizing Modern Languages' (http://www.transnationalmodernlanguages.ac.uk/).

In 2017, Shirin published the English translation in a printed form of *Clouds over the Equator – The forgotten Italians*.

Made in the USA
Columbia, SC
29 April 2017